Book 1
Android Programming In a Day!
BY SAM KEY

&

Book 2
JavaScript Professional Programming Made Easy
BY SAM KEY

Book 1
Android Programming In a Day!
BY SAM KEY

The Power Guide for Beginners In Android App Programming

**Programming Box Set #79: Android Programming in a Day &
JavaScript Professional Made Easy**

Table Of Contents

Introduction

I want to thank you and congratulate you for purchasing the book, "Introduction to Android Programming in a Day – The Power Guide for Beginners in Android App Programming".

This book contains proven steps and strategies on how to get started with Android app development.

This book will focus on preparing you with the fun and tiring world of Android app development. Take note that this book will not teach you on how to program. It will revolve around the familiarization of the Android SDK and Eclipse IDE.

Why not focus on programming immediately? Unfortunately, the biggest reason many aspiring Android developers stop on learning this craft is due to the lack of wisdom on the Android SDK and Eclipse IDE.

Sure, you can also make apps using other languages like Python and other IDEs on the market. However, you can expect that it is much more difficult than learning Android's SDK and Eclipse's IDE.

On the other hand, you can use tools online to develop your Android app for you. But where's the fun in that? You will not learn if you use such tools. Although it does not mean that you should completely stay away from that option.

Anyway, the book will be split into four chapters. The first will prepare you and tell you the things you need before you develop apps. The second will tell you how you can configure your project. The third will introduce you to the Eclipse IDE. And the last chapter will teach you on how to run your program in your Android device.

Also, this book will be sprinkled with tidbits about the basic concepts of Android app development. And as you read along, you will have an idea on what to do next.

Thanks again for purchasing this book, I hope you enjoy it!

Chapter 1: Preparation

Android application development is not easy. You must have some decent background in program development. It is a plus if you know Visual Basic and Java. And it will be definitely a great advantage if you are familiar or have already used Eclipse's IDE (Integrated Development Environment). Also, being familiar with XML will help you.

You will need a couple of things before you can start developing apps.

First, you will need a high-end computer. It is common that other programming development kits do not need a powerful computer in order to create applications. However, creating programs for Android is a bit different. You will need more computing power for you to run Android emulators, which are programs that can allow you to test your programs in your computer.

Using a weak computer without a decent processor and a good amount of RAM will only make it difficult for you to run those emulators. If you were able to run it, it will run slowly.

Second, you will need an Android device. That device will be your beta tester. With it, you will know how your program will behave in an Android device. When choosing the test device, make sure that it is at par with the devices of the market you are targeting for your app. If you are targeting tablet users, use a tablet. If you are targeting smartphones, then use a smartphone.

Third, you will need the Android SDK (Software Development Kit) from Google. The SDK is a set of files and programs that can allow you to create and compile your program's code. As of this writing, the

latest Android SDK's file size is around 350mb. It will take you 15 –
30 minutes to download it. If you uncompressed the Android SDK
file, it will take up around 450mb of your computer's disk space. The
link   to   the   download   page   is:
http://developer.android.com/sdk/index.html

The SDK can run on Windows XP, Windows 7, Mac OSX 10.8.5 (or
higher), and Linux distros that can run 32bit applications and has
glibc (GNU C library) 2.11 or higher.

Once you have unpacked the contents of the file you downloaded,
open the SDK Manager. That program is the development kit's update
tool. To make sure you have the latest versions of the kit's
components, run the manager once in a while and download those
updates. Also, you can use the SDK Manager to download older
versions of SDK. You must do that in case you want to make
programs with devices with dated Android operating systems.

Chapter 2: Starting Your First Project

To start creating programs, you will need to open Eclipse. The Eclipse application file can be found under the eclipse folder on the extracted files from the Android SDK. Whenever you run Eclipse, it will ask you where you want your Eclipse workspace will be stored. You can just use the default location and just toggle the don't show checkbox.

New Project

To start a new Android application project, just click on the dropdown button of the New button on Eclipse's toolbar. A context menu will appear, and click on the Android application project.

The New Android Application project details window will appear. In there, you will need to input some information for your project. You must provide your program's application name, project name, and package name. Also, you can configure the minimum and target SDK where your program can run and the SDK that will be used to compile your code. And lastly, you can indicate the default theme that your program will use.

Application Name

The application name will be the name that will be displayed on the Google's Play Store when you post it there. The project name will be more of a file name for Eclipse. It will be the project's identifier. It should be unique for every project that you build in Eclipse. By default, Eclipse will generate a project and package name for your project when you type something in the Application Name text box.

Package Name

The package name is not usually displayed for users. Take note that in case you will develop a large program, you must remember that your package name should never be changed. On the other hand, it is common that package names are the reverse of your domain name plus your project's name. For example, if your website's domain name is www.mywebsite.com and your project's name is Hello World, a good package name for your project will be com.mywebsite.helloworld.

The package name should follow the Java package name convention. The naming convention is there to prevent users from having similar names, which could result to numerous conflicts. Some of the rules you need to follow for the package name are:

• Your package name should be all in lower caps. Though Eclipse will accept a package name with a capital letter, but it is still best to adhere to standard practice.

• The reverse domain naming convention is included as a standard practice.

• Avoid using special characters in the package name. Instead, you can replace it with underscores.

• Also, you should never use or include the default com.example in your package name. Google Play will not accept an app with a package name like that.

Minimum SDK

Minimum required SDK could be set to lower or the lowest version of Android. Anything between the latest and the set minimum required version can run your program. Setting it to the lowest, which is API 1 or Android 1.0, can make your target audience wider.

Setting it to Android 2.2 (Froyo) or API 8, can make your program run on almost 95% of all Android devices in the world. The drawback fn this is that the features you can include in your program will be limited. Adding new features will force your minimum required SDK to move higher since some of the new functions in Android is not available on lower versions of the API (Application Programming Interface).

Target SDK

The target SDK should be set to the version of Android that most of your target audience uses. It indicates that you have tested your program to that version. And it means that your program is fully functional if they use it on a device that runs the target Android version.

Whenever a new version of Android appears, you should also update the target SDK of your program. Of course, before you release it to the market again, make sure that you test it on an updated device.

If a device with the same version as your set target SDK runs your program, it will not do any compatibility behavior or adjust itself to run the program. By default, you should set it to the highest version to attract your potential app buyers. Setting a lower version for your target SDK would make your program old and dated. By the way, the target SDK should be always higher or equal with the minimum target SDK version.

Compile with

The compile with version should be set to the latest version of Android. This is to make sure that your program will run on almost all versions down to the minimum version you have indicated, and to take advantage of the newest features and optimization offered by the latest version of Android. By default, the Android SDK will only have one version available for this option, which is API 20 or Android 4.4 (KitKat Wear).

After setting those all up, it is time to click on the Next button. The
new page in the screen will contain some options such as creating
custom launcher icon and creating activity. As of now, you do not
need to worry about those. Just leave the default values and check,
and click the Next button once again.

Custom Launcher Icon

Since you have left the Create Custom Launcher option checked, the
next page will bring you in the launcher icon customization page. In
there, you will be given three options on how you would create your
launcher. Those options are launcher icons made from an image,
clipart, or text.

With the text and clipart method, you can easily create an icon you
want without thinking about the size and quality of the launcher icon.
With those two, you can just get a preset image from the SDK or
Android to use as a launcher icon. The same goes with the text
method since all you need is to type the letters you want to appear on
the icon and the SDK will generate an icon based on that.

The launcher icon editor also allows you to change the background
and foreground color of your icon. Also, you can scale the text and
clipart by changing the value of the additional padding of the icon.
And finally, you can add simple 3D shapes on your icon to make it
appear more professional.

Bitmap Iconography Tips

When it comes to images, you need to take note of a few reminders.
First, always make sure that you will use vector images. Unlike the
typical bitmap images (pictures taken from cameras or images
created using Paint), vector images provide accurate and sharp
images. You can scale it multiple times, but its sharpness will not
disappear and will not pixelate. After all, vector images do not contain
information about pixels. It only has numbers and location of the

colors and lines that will appear in it. When it is scaled, it does not perform antialiasing or stretching since its image will be mathematically rendered.

In case that you will be the one creating or designing the image that you will use for your program and you will be creating a bitmap image, make sure that you start with a large image. A large image is easier to create and design.

Also, since in Android, multiple sizes of your icon will be needed, a large icon can make it easier for you to make smaller ones. Take note that if you scale a big picture into a small one, some details will be lost, but it will be easier to edit and fix and it will still look crisp. On the other hand, if you scale a small image into a big one, it will pixelate and insert details that you do not intend to show such as jagged and blurred edges.

Nevertheless, even when scaling down a big image into a smaller one, do not forget to rework the image. Remember that a poor-looking icon makes people think that the app you are selling is low-quality. And again, if you do not want to go through all that, create a vector image instead.

Also, when you create an image, make sure that it will be visible in any background. Aside from that, it is advisable to make it appear uniform with other Android icons. To do that, make sure that your image has a distinct silhouette that will make it look like a 3D image. The icon should appear as if you were looking above it and as if the source of light is on top of the image. The topmost part of the icon should appear lighter and the bottom part should appear darker.

Activity

Once you are done with your icon, click on the Next button. The page will now show the Activity window. It will provide you with activity templates to work on. The window has a preview box where you can see what your app will look like for every activity template. Below the selection, there is a description box that will tell you what each template does. For now, select the Blank Activity and click Next. The next page will ask you some details regarding the activity. Leave it on its default values and click Finish.

Once you do that, Eclipse will setup your new project. It might take a lot of time, especially if you are using a dated computer. The next chapter will discuss the programming interface of Eclipse.

Chapter 3: Getting Familiar with Eclipse and Contents of an Android App

When Eclipse has finished its preparation, you will be able to start doing something to your program. But hold onto your horses; explore Eclipse first before you start fiddling with anything.

Editing Area

In the middle of the screen, you will see a preview of your program. In it, you will see your program's icon beside the title of your program. Just left of it is the palette window. It contains all the elements that you can place in your program.

Both of these windows are inside Eclipse's editing area. You will be spending most of your time here, especially if you are going to edit or view something in your code or layout.

The form widgets tab will be expanded in the palette by default. There you will see the regular things you see in an Android app such as buttons, radio buttons, progress bar (the circle icon that spins when something is loading in your device or the bar the fills up when your device is loading), seek bar, and the ratings bar (the stars you see in reviews).

Aside from the form widgets, there are other elements that you can check and use. Press the horizontal tabs or buttons and examine all the elements you can possibly use in your program.

To insert a widget in your program, you can just drag the element you want to include from the palette and drop it in your program's preview. Eclipse will provide you visual markers and grid snaps for

you to place the widgets you want on the exact place you want. Easy,
right?

Take note, some of the widgets on the palette may require higher-
level APIs or versions of Android. For example, the Grid Layout from
the Layouts section of the palette requires API 14 (Android 4.0 Ice
Cream Sandwich) or higher. If you add it in your program, it will ask
you if you want to install it. In case you did include and install it,
remember that it will not be compatible for older versions or any
device running on API 13 and lower. It is advisable that you do not
include any element that asks for installation. It might result into
errors.

Output Area, Status Bar, and Problem Browser

On the bottom part of Eclipse, the status bar, problem browser, and
output area can be found. It will contain messages regarding to the
state of your project. If Eclipse found errors in your program, it will
be listed there. Always check the Problems bar for any issues. Take
note that you cannot run or compile your program if Eclipse finds at
least one error on your project.

Navigation Pane

On the leftmost part of your screen is the navigation pane that
contains the package explorer. The package explorer lets you browse
all the files that are included in your project. Three of the most
important files that you should know where to look for are:

• activity_main.xml: This file is your program's main page or
window. And it will be the initial file that will be opened when you
create a new project. In case you accidentally close it on your editor
window, you can find it at: YourProjectName > res > layout >
activity_main.xml.

• MainActivity.java: As of now, you will not need to touch this file. However, it is important to know where it is since later in your Android development activities, you will need to understand it and its contents. It is located at: YourProjectName > src > YourPackageName > MainActivity.java.

• AndroidManifest.xml: It contains the essential information that you have set up a while ago when you were creating your project file in Eclipse. You can edit the minimum and target SDK in there. It is located at YourProjectName > AndroidManifest.xml.

Aside from those files, you should take note of the following directories:

• src/: This is where most of your program's source files will be placed. And your main activity file is locafile is located.

• res/: Most of the resources will be placed here. The resources are placed inside the subdirectories under this folder.

• res/drawable-hdpi/: Your high density bitmap files that you might show in your app will go in here.

• res/layout/: All the pages or interface in your app will be located here – including your activity_main.xml.

• res/values/: The values you will store and use in your program will be placed in this directory in form of XML files.

**Programming Box Set #79: Android Programming in a Day &
JavaScript Professional Made Easy**

In the event that you will create multiple projects, remember that the directory for those other projects aside from the one you have opened will still be available in your package explorer. Because of that, you might get confused over the files you are working on. Thankfully, Eclipse's title bar indicates the location and name of the file you are editing, which makes it easier to know what is currently active on the editing area.

Outline Box

Displays the current structure of the file you are editing. The outline panel will help you visualize the flow and design of your app. Also, it can help you find the widgets you want to edit.

Properties Box

Whenever you are editing a layout file, the properties box will appear below the outline box. With the properties box, you can edit certain characteristics of a widget. For example, if you click on the Hello World text on the preview of your main activity layout file, the contents of the properties box will be populated. In there, you can edit the properties of the text element that you have clicked. You can change the text, height, width, and even its font color.

Menu and Toolbar

The menu bar contains all the major functionalities of Eclipse. In case you do not know where the button of a certain tool is located, you can just invoke that tool's function on the menu bar. On the other hand, the tool bar houses all the major functions in Eclipse. The most notable buttons there are the New, Save, and Run.

As of now, look around Eclipse's interface. Also, do not do or change anything on the main activity file or any other file. The next chapter will discuss about how to run your program. As of now, the initial contents of your project are also valid as an android program. Do not change anything since you might produce an unexpected error. Nevertheless, if you really do want to change something, go ahead. You can just create another project for you to keep up with the next chapter.

Chapter 4: Running Your Program

By this time, even if you have not done anything yet to your program, you can already run and test it in your Android device or emulator. Why teach this first before the actual programming? Well, unlike typical computer program development, Android app development is a bit bothersome when it comes to testing.

First, the program that you are developing is intended for Android devices. You cannot actually run it normally in your computer without the help of an emulator. And you will actually do a lot of testing. Even with the first lines of code or changes in your program, you will surely want to test it.

Second, the Android emulator works slow. Even with good computers, the emulator that comes with the Android SDK is painstakingly sluggish. Alternatively, you can use BlueStacks. BlueStacks is a free Android emulator that works better than the SDK's emulator. It can even run games with it! However, it is buggy and does not work well (and does not even run sometimes) with every computer.

This chapter will focus on running your program into your Android device. You will need to have a USB data cable and connect your computer and Android. Also, you will need to have the right drivers for your device to work as a testing platform for the programs you will develop. Unfortunately, this is the preferred method for most beginners since running your app on Android emulators can bring a lot more trouble since it is super slow. And that might even discourage you to continue Android app development.

Why Android Emulators are Slow

Why are Android emulators slow? Computers can run virtual OSs without any problems, but why cannot the Android emulator work fine? Running virtual OSs is not something as resource-extensive anymore with today's computer standards. However, with Android, you will actually emulate an OS together with a mobile device. And nowadays, these mobile devices are as powerful as some of the dated computers back then. Regular computers will definitely have a hard time with that kind of payload from an Android emulator.

USB Debugging Mode

To run your program in an Android device, connect your Android to your computer. After that, set your Android into USB debugging mode. Depending on the version of the Android device you are using, the steps might change.

For 3.2 and older Android devices:

Go to Settings > Applications > Development

For 4.0 and newer Android devices:

Go to Settings > Developer Options

For 4.2 and newer Android devices with hidden Developer Options:

Go to Settings > About Phone. After that, tap the Build Number seven times. Go back to the previous screen. The Developer Options should be visible now.

Android Device Drivers

When USB debugging is enabled, your computer will install the right drivers for the Android device that you have. If your computer does not have the right drivers, you will not be able to run your program on

your device. If that happens to you, visit this page:
http://developer.android.com/tools/extras/oem-usb.html.   It
contains instructions on how you can install the right driver for your
device and operating system.

Running an App in Your Android Device Using Eclipse

Once your device is already connected and you have the right drivers
for it, you can now do a test run of your application. On your Eclipse
window, click the Run button on the toolbar or in the menu bar.

If a Run As window appeared, select the Android Application option
and click on the OK button. After that, a dialog box will appear. It will
provide you with two options: running the program on an Android
device or on an AVD (Android Virtual Device) or emulator.

If your device was properly identified by your computer, it will appear
on the list. Click on your device's name and click OK. Eclipse will
compile your Android app, install it on your device, and then run it.
That is how simple it is.

Take note, there will be times that your device will appear offline on
the list. In case that happens, there are two simple fixes that you can
do to make it appear online again: restart your device or disable and
enable the USB debugging function on your device.

Now, you can start placing widgets on your main activity file.
However, always make sure that you do not place any widgets that
require higher APIs.

Conclusion

Thank you again for purchasing this book!

I hope this book was able to help you get started with Android Programming in a Day!.

The next step is to study the following:

View and Viewgroups: View and Viewgroups are the two types of objects that you will be dealing with Android. View objects are the elements or widgets that you see in Android programs. Viewgroup objects act as containers to those View objects.

Relative, Linear, and Table Layout: When it comes to designing your app, you need to know the different types of layouts. In later versions of Android, you can use other versions of layouts, but of course, the API requirements will go up if you use them. Master these, and you will be able to design faster and cleaner.

Adding Activities or Interface: Of course, you would not want your program to contain one page only. You need more. You must let your app customers to see more content and functions. In order to do that, you will need to learn adding activities to your program. This is the part when developing your Android app will be tricky. You will not be able to rely completely on the drag and drop function and graphical layout view of Eclipse. You will need to start typing some code into your program.

Adding the Action Bar: The action bar is one of the most useful elements in Android apps. It provides the best location for the most used functions in your program. And it also aid your users when switching views, tabs, or drop down list.

Once you have gain knowledge on those things, you will be able to launch a decent app on the market. The last thing you might want to do is to learn how to make your program support other Android devices.

You must know very well that Android devices come in all shapes and form. An Android device can be a tablet, a smartphone, or even a television. Also, they come with different screen sizes. You cannot just expect that all your customers will be using a 4-inch display smartphone. Also, you should think about the versions of Android they are using. Lastly, you must also add language options to your programs. Even though English is fine, some users will appreciate if your program caters to the primary language that they use.

And that is about it for this book. Make sure you do not stop learning Android app development.

Finally, if you enjoyed this book, please take the time to share your thoughts and post a review on Amazon. We do our best to reach out to readers and provide the best value we can. Your positive review will help us achieve that. It'd be greatly appreciated!

Thank you and good luck!

Book 2
JavaScript Professional Programming Made Easy

BY SAM KEY

Expert JavaScripts Programming Language Success in a Day for Any Computer User!

**Programming Box Set #79: Android Programming in a Day &
JavaScript Professional Made Easy**

Table Of Contents

Introduction

I want to thank you and congratulate you for purchasing the book, "Professional JavaScript Programming Made Easy: Expert JavaScripts Programming Language Success In A Day for Any Computer User!"

This book contains proven steps and strategies on how to code JavaScript from scratch.

This book will give you a solid idea on how JavaScript works and how it can be applied to your web pages. This is an ideal book that every beginner should read. However, it is required that you already know HTML and CSS.

Familiarity with other programming languages such as Java, Visual Basic, and C is a plus since it will make it easier for you to learn and understand the concepts behind the processes involved in coding JavaScript.

Every explanation in the book will be accompanied by an example. Those examples will be shown in Courier New font; in case that font is not available, it will be shown in a monospaced generic family font instead.

To learn and code JavaScript, all you need is a text editing tool such as Notepad in Windows or TextEdit in Macintosh computers. However, it is recommend that you use a source code editor or a text editing tool with syntax highlighting that supports HTML, CSS, and JavaScript languages to speed up your learning and reduce the typos you will make.

One of the best and free source code editor tools you can get from the internet is Notepad++. It will be discussed in the last chapter of the book.

Thanks again for purchasing this book, I hope you enjoy it!

Chapter 1: Introduction to JavaScript

JavaScript is a scripting or programming language that is mainly used for web pages. Almost all websites use it to provide their visitors a richer browsing experience. Compared to coding HTML, JavaScript is real programming.

It is safe to say that JavaScript is the most popular and most widely used programming language in the world. JavaScript is easy to learn, and that is why web developers or even hobbyists can use it after a few days of studying it.

Unlike other programming languages, JavaScript is easy to learn and apply practically. The programs or scripts created from JavaScript are used by millions of people – even though they do not know they are already using them.

JavaScript can turn your old HTML files, which are static, into dynamic. You can embed JavaScript into your files for you to deliver web pages with dynamic content and appearance.

To embed JavaScript to your HTML file, you must enclose your script inside script HTML tags (<script></script>). Commonly, you should place the script tags inside the head HTML tags (<head></head>). However, there will be times that you might want or need to place them inside your page's body (<body></body>).

On the other hand, JavaScript can be placed in an external file and linked on a web page to work. It will be considered to be a part of the HTML file being parsed by the browser once it is linked.

Client and Server Side Scripting

In web development, JavaScript is termed as a client side scripting language. All the scripts that you write in JavaScript are executed on the client side, which is your or your visitors' browser.

On the other hand, PHP and ASP are server side scripting languages. As you might have guessed, the scripts or programs created using those two are executed on the server and their results are usually sent to the client.

The two complete the concept of DHTML (Dynamic HTML). When you use client and server side scripting, your pages will become more dynamic and interactive. With them, you can create social media websites, online games, and even your own search engine. And those statements are not exaggerated. You are truly a few steps away from greatness once you master JavaScript and a server side scripting language.

However, take note that learning client side scripting is a prerequisite before learning server side scripting. After all, most of the functions and features that you will create using server side scripting will require or need the support of client side scripting. Also, client side scripting is a good introduction to programming for web developers who have no experience or even any idea on how programming works.

Before you start learning and applying JavaScript to your web documents, you should learn and master HTML and CSS. In JavaScript, you will be mostly dealing with HTML elements, so it is a requirement that you know about HTML elements and attributes.

Alternatively, if you want to use JavaScript to perform advanced styling on your document such as animations and dynamic layouts, then you should have a solid background on CSS.

To give you a short summary of the relationship between HTML, CSS, and JavaScript, take note of these pointers:

- HTML is used to define the content and elements of your web page.

- CSS is used to specify or precisely define the appearance and layout of your web page.

- JavaScript is used to create functionalities in your web page. It can also be used to define content like HTML and define appearances like CSS.

With JavaScript, you can fully control everything on your web page. You can change an HTML element's content. For example, you can change the text content of a paragraph element with JavaScript.

You can also change the value of one of the attributes of an HTML element. For example, you can change the HREF attribute of a link you inserted on your document.

And lastly, you can change the CSS or styling values of an HTML element. For example, you can change the font-weight of one of your headers in your web document with JavaScript, too.

Also, with JavaScript, you have full control on when it will be applied, unlike CSS. You can run your scripts before the page loads, while the page is loading, after the page loaded, and while your user browses the page.

On the other hand, you can make those changes automatic or triggered by the visitor. You can add other factors such as time of the day, specific user actions, or user browsing behavior to trigger those changes or functions.

Chapter 2: HTML DOM and Assigning Values

How can JavaScript do all of that? It can do all of that because it takes advantage of the HTML DOM or Document Object Model. JavaScript can access, modify, and remove any HTML element together with its properties by using HTML DOM.

Assigning Attribute Values with JavaScript

With CSS, you have dealt with selectors. By using the right selector, you can change the CSS style of a specific element, group or class of elements, group of similar elements, handpicked elements, or all of the elements in your page. By this point, you must already know how id's and classes works.

JavaScript almost works like that, too. To change the content of an element, value of an element's property or attribute, or style of an element, you will need to select them first and assign a value. Below is an example of using JavaScript to change a paragraph element's (which has a value of "testparagraph" for its id attribute) font size:

```
<head>
<script>
document.getElementById("testparagraph"
).style.fontSize = "17px";
</script>
</head>
<body>
<p id='testparagraph' >This a paragraph. This is another sentence. This is the last sentence.</p>
</body>
```

The previous line's equivalent to CSS is:

#testparagraph {font-size: 17px;}

They have different syntax, but they will have the same result. In the CSS example, the paragraph with the "testparagraph" id was selected by placing a pound sign and typing the id value.

In JavaScript, "testparagraph" was selected using DOM. If you will translate the example JavaScript line to plain English, the line says to the browser that the line of code pertains to something or will do something within the document, which is your webpage.

Then the next part tells the browser that you are looking for a certain element that has a value of "testparagraph" on its id attribute. The next part tells the browser that you will do something to the style attribute of the "testparagraph" element. And the last part tells the browser that you will assign a value on the fontSize within the element's style attribute.

In JavaScript, the equals sign (=) means that you will assign a value to the variable or property on its left. And the value that you will assign on the variable or property is on the right.

On the example, you will assign the value "17px" to the fontSize style attribute of the element "testparagraph" that is located within your HTML document. The semicolon at the end tells the browser that it is the end of the line for that code, and it should parse the next line for it to execute.

Browser Parsing Behavior

By default, that previous JavaScript example will not work. The reason is that browsers read and execute HTML documents line by line – from the starting tag of the html tag, the browser will perform scripts, apply CSS values, place the HTML elements, place their specific contents, etcetera, until the browser reach the closing html tag.

In the example, the line asks the browser for an element that has the value "testparagraph" in its id attribute in the document. Unfortunately, the browser has not reached the body of the document where the definition of the element "testparagraph" resides.

Because of that, the browser will return an error saying that there is no element that has that attribute. You cannot assign a value for the attribute font size style to a nonexistent or null object. Hence, when the browser reaches the definition of the element "testparagraph", its font size will not be changed to the value you have set in the JavaScript code.

The solution to that is simple: you can place the script after the part where the element "testparagraph" was defined, and that is any location after the closing paragraph of the element "testparagraph".

Chapter 3: JavaScript Statements

In the last part of the previous chapter, the book loosely discussed about how browsers read HTML files and JavaScript lines and how you can assign values to an attribute. This chapter will supplement you with further discussions about that and JavaScript statements.

To construct a program using a programming language, you will need to write lines of codes. Those lines of codes are called statements. A statement is a line of code that contains an instruction for the computer to execute. In JavaScript, the one that executes the code is your internet browser.

Statements in JavaScript might contain the following: Keywords, Expressions, Operators, Comments, and Values. Below are sample lines of JavaScript that this chapter will dissect; this is done so that you will know the parts that comprise JavaScript statements:

var x; // This is a comment line.
var y; // To create one, you must place two forward slashes.
var z; // Comment lines are ignored by the browser.
x = 1 + 1; // So you can place them before or after a statement.
y = "Hello World." // And it will not affect the syntax.
z = 10 // But do not put them in the middle of a statement.
Keywords

In the example, the word var is a keyword. Typically, keywords are reserved words that you cannot use in your program except when you need to use their purpose. In the sample statements, the keyword var tells the browser to create a variable named x. Variables will be discussed later.

Expressions

On the other hand, 1 + 1 is an expression and the + and = sign are examples of operators. Expressions, in computer programming, are combinations of operators, values, constants, and variables that will be interpreted by the computer to produce a result. In x = 1 + 1, the browser will compute or evaluate that expression and return a value of 2. Expressions are not limited to arithmetic operations in JavaScript. Expressions can be in form of Boolean comparison, string operations, and etcetera.

Values

There are two values types that you will see and use in JavaScript. The first type is fixed or literal values; the second type is variables.

Literal Values

Numbers, Strings (text enclosed in single or double quotes), and even Expressions are literal values. In the example, the parts "Hello World" (string), 10 (number), and 1 + 1 (expression) are literal values.

Variables

On the other hand, variables are data containers. Variables can contain literal values such as strings, numbers, arrays, expressions, and even objects.

To use or create one, you must name it or create an identifier for it. Identifiers are combinations of letters, underscores, and dollar signs and must not be the same with any keywords or reserved words in JavaScript.

However, take note that identifiers must start with a letter, an underscore, or a dollar sign only. Starting with a number will return an error, and including symbols other than underscores and dollar signs will not be accepted by JavaScript.

Local Variable and Global Variables

There are two types of variables in JavaScript. The first one is local and the second one is global. The type of variable depends on where it was declared. The difference between them is how they are handled in the script.

Variables that are declared outside of functions will become a global variable. And variables that are declared inside functions will become a local variable.

Global variables will stay on the memory until the web page is closed. It can be referenced and used anywhere in the script. On the other hand, local variables will only stay on the memory until the browser finishes executing the function where the variable was declared. It can be only referenced and used by the function where it was declared. Functions will be discussed later in this book.

In the sample JavaScript statements, the letters x, y, and z are global variables.

To create a variable in JavaScript, you must use the var keyword – just like in the previous example. To assign values to them, you can use the equal operator.

Operators

There are multiple of operators that you can use in JavaScript. And it can be categorized into the following:

- Arithmetic

- Assignment

- String

- Comparison

- Logical

- Conditional

- Bitwise

- Typeof

- Delete Unary +

Only the first four types of operators are mostly the ones that you will frequently use during your early days of JavaScript programming: Arithmetic, Assignment, String, and Comparison. The remaining operators are typically used for advanced projects and might be confusing for beginners.

On the other hand, take note that some of the operator symbols may serve two purposes or more. For example, the + sign can be used as an arithmetic, string, or unary + operator depending on the condition or your goal.

Comments

You might already have an idea on what comments are. As mentioned before, they are ignored by browsers, and their only function is to serve as reminders or notes for you – just like the comments in HTML. You can create a new line of comment by using two forward slashes. If you want to create a block of comment, start it with /* and end it with */.

Chapter 4: JavaScript's Basic Syntax

For the browser to execute a JavaScript statement, the statement must follow the correct syntax and must only have one instruction (this may vary depending the code).

Just a small mistake in the syntax will make the computer do something different from what you want to happen or it might not do nothing and return an error.

If you have a large block of code and one of the statements gets an error, the browser will not execute the lines that follow the statement that generated an error.

Due to that, it is important that you always check your code and avoid creating mistakes to make sure that you will achieve the things you want to happen with JavaScript.

JavaScript Syntax

JavaScript, just like other computer languages, follow syntax. In computer programming, syntax is a set of rules that you must follow when writing codes.

One of the syntax rules in JavaScript is to terminate each statement with a colon. It is like placing a dot in every sentence you make.

This rule is flexible due to ASI (Automatic Semicolon Inserting). Even if you do not place a semicolon at the end of your statement, once you start a new line, the previous line will be considered as a complete statement – as if it has a semicolon at the end. However, not placing semicolons is bad practice since it might produce bugs and errors.

Another rule is to make sure that you close brackets, parentheses, and quotations in your code. For example, leaving a dangling curly brace will result in an error. And with quotation marks, if you started with a single quote, end it with a single quote. If you start with a double quote, end with a double quote.

Take note that JavaScript is a case-sensitive language. Unlike HTML wherein you can use lower, upper, and mixed case on tags and attributes, JavaScript will return an error once you use the wrong case for a method or variable. For example, changing the capitalization of the letter b in the getElementById will result to an error.

Never create variables that have the similar name with keywords or reserved words. Also, always declare variables. If you do not explicitly declare them and use them on your statements, you might get unexpected results or a reference error. For example:

var y;

var z;

y = 1;

z = 1 + x;

Once your browser reads the last line, no value will be assigned to z because the browser will return a reference error.

That is just a few of the rules in JavaScript's syntax. Some methods and keywords follow certain syntax. Remember them to prevent yourself from the hassle of unneeded debugging.

Chapter 5: Functions and Events

You already know by now what statements are and how to write statements in accordance to JavaScript's syntax rules. You also know how to assign values to an HTML element's attribute by using JavaScript. In this chapter, you will know how to create functions or methods.

A function is a block of statements that you can call or invoke anytime to execute. In other programming languages, functions are called subroutines, methods, or procedures. The statements inside a function will not be immediately executed when the browser parses the HTML document. It will only run or be executed if it is called or invoked.

Purposes of Functions

What are the purposes of functions? First, it allows you to control when to execute a block of statements as explained previously.

Second, it allows you to create 'mini' programs in your script. For example, if you want to make a paragraph to be centered align, to have a heavier font, and to have a bigger font size when you click the paragraph, you can create a function for that goal and capture an event that will trigger that function once you click on the paragraph.

Third, creating functions is a good way to separate lengthy blocks of statements into smaller chunks. Maintaining and debugging your script will be much easier with functions.

Fourth, it can effectively lessen redundancy in your script. Instead of writing the same sequence of statements repeatedly in your script, you can just create a function, and just call it again when you need the browser to execute the statements within it once more.

Creating Functions

To create a function, you will need to use the keyword function. When you create a function you must follow a simple syntax. Below is an example of a function:

function MakeBolderAndBigger(elementID) {

**document.getElementById(elementID).style.fontSize = "20px";
document.getElementById(elementID).style.fontWeight = "20px";
}**

In the example, the keyword function was followed with MakeBolderAndBigger. That part is the function's name. Naming a function has the same rules with naming a variable identifier.

After the function's name, there is elementID which is enclosed in parentheses. That part of the function is called a parameter. You can place as many parameters that you want or none at all. If you place multiple parameters, you must separate them with a comma and a space. If you are not going to use parameters, just leave it blank but never forget to place the parentheses.

A parameter stores that value or the function arguments that was placed on it when the function is invoked. That parameter will act as local variable in the function. This part will be discussed further later.

Then, after the parameter, you will see a curly brace. And after the statements, there is another curly brace.

The first brace act as a sign that tells the browsers that any statements following it is a code block for the function. The second brace tells the browsers that the code block is finished, and any line of code after it is not related to the function. Those are the rules you need to follow when creating a function.

Invoking Functions

There are two common ways to invoke a function. First, you can invoke it within your script. Second, you can invoke it by placing and triggering event handlers.

Invoke within Code

The first method of invoking functions is easy. All you need to do is to type the name of the function, and fill in the arguments that the function's parameters require. To invoke the example function using the first method, you can simply type this:

MakeBolderAndBigger("testparagraph");

Once your browser reads that, it will process the function. Since you have placed "testparagraph" as the argument for the parameter elementID, elementID will have a value of "testparagraph". It will now act as a variable.

When the browser executes the first statement in the function, which is document.getElementById(elementID).style.fontSize = "20px";, it will select the element "testparagraph" and change its font size value to 20px.

On the other hand, you can actually provide no argument for function parameters. If you do this instead:

MakeBolderAndBigger();

The browser will execute the function. However, since you did not store any value to the parameter, the parameter elementID will be undefined and will have the value undefined.

Because of that, when the first statement tries to look for the element with the id attribute of elementID, which has the value of undefined, it will return an error.

Once the browser finishes executing the function, it will return on reading the next line of code after the function invocation. For example:

MakeBolderAndBigger("testparagraph"); document.getElementById("testparagraph").style.color = "blue";

After the browser finishes executing the function MakeBolderAndBigger, it will proceed on executing the next statement below and make the font color of "testparagraph" to blue. The example above is the same as coding:

document.getElementById("testparagraph").style.fontSize = "20px"; document.getElementById("testparagraph").style.fontWeight = "20px"; document.getElementById("testparagraph").style.color = "blue";

Invoke with Events

Every action that a user does in a web page and every action that the browser performs are considered events. A few of those events are:

- When the page finishes loading

- When a user or script changes the content of a text field

- When a user click a button or an HTML element

- When a user presses on a keyboard key

To invoke a function when an event happens, you must tell the browser by placing some piece of codes in your page's HTML. Below is an example:

<button onClick='MakeBolderAndBigger("testparagraph");' >Invoke Function</button>

When a user clicks on that button element, it will trigger the function MakeBolderAndBigger. The syntax for that is simple. Just insert the event inside the opening tag of an HTML element that has the event that you want to capture, place an equal sign, place the function that you want to execute together with the arguments you need to place on it, and then enclose the function in quotes.

By the way, be wary of quotes. If you used a single quote to enclose the function, then use double quotes to enclose the values on your arguments. Just think of it as if you are assigning values on an element's style attribute in HTML. Also, as best practice, never forget to place a semicolon at the end.

As a reference, below are some of the events that you can use in HTML and JavaScript:

- onClick – triggers when the user clicks on the HTML element

- onMouseOver – triggers when the user hovers on the HTML element

- onMouseOut – triggers when the user's mouse pointers move out from the element's display

- onKeyDown – triggers when the user presses a keyboard key

- onChange – triggers when the user changes the content of a text field

- onLoad – triggers when the browser is done loading the body, images, frames, and other scripts

Chapter 6: Debugging, Text Editing Tool, and References

In modern browsers, most of JavaScript errors are handled automatically and ignored to prevent browsing disruption. So when testing your scripts when opening your HTML files on a browser, it is difficult to spot errors and debug.

Web Developer Consoles on Browsers

Fortunately, a few of those browsers have built-in developer consoles where you can monitor errors and the resources that your page generates and uses. One of those browsers that have this functionality is Google Chrome. To access its developer console, you can press F12 on your keyboard while a page is open on it.

Pressing the key will open the developer tools panel within Chrome, and you can click on the Console tab to monitor the errors that your page generates. Aside from monitoring errors, you can use it to test statements, check the values of your variables, call functions, etc.

Text Editing Tool with Syntax Highlighting

You can get away with a few problems when writing HTML and CSS on typical text editing tools like Notepad. However, with JavaScript coding, using those ordinary tools is a challenge. Unlike the two, JavaScript has a strict and vast syntax. Just one typo in your script and you will start hunting bugs after you test the statements you wrote. After all, it is a programming language unlike HTML which is a markup language.

To make your life easier, it is best that you use a text editing tool with syntax highlighting when coding JavaScript. One of the best tools out there on the Web is Notepad++. It is free and it is as lightweight (in terms of resource usage) and as simple as Notepad.

The syntax highlighting will help you spot missing brackets and quotation marks. It will also prevent you from using keywords as variables since keywords are automatically highlighted in a different color, which will help you realize sooner that they are identifiers you cannot use for variables.

References

As of now, you have only learned the basics of how to code JavaScript. You might have been itching to change the values of other attributes in your HTML code, but you do not know the HTML DOM to use. On the other hand, you might be interested on knowing the other operators that you can use in your script.

The book has omitted most of them since it focused more on the coding process in JavaScript. Thankfully, you can just look up those values and operators on the net. To give you a head start, this a link to the JavaScript reference list made by the developers in the Mozilla Foundation: https://developer.mozilla.org/en-US/docs/Web/JavaScript/Reference.

Conclusion

Thank you again for purchasing this book!

I hope this book was able to help you to learn the basics of coding with JavaScript.

The next step is to:

Master the HTML DOM.

Become familiar with other keywords and their usage.

Finally, if you enjoyed this book, please take the time to share your thoughts and post a review on Amazon. We do our best to reach out to readers and provide the best value we can. Your positive review will help us achieve that. It'd be greatly appreciated!

Thank you and good luck!

Check Out My Other Books

Below you'll find some of my other popular books that are popular on Amazon and Kindle as well. Simply click on the links below to check them out. Alternatively, you can visit my author page on Amazon to see other work done by me.

C Programming Success in a Day

Android Programming in a Day

C ++ Programming Success in a Day

C Programming Professional Made Easy

Python Programming in a Day

PHP Programming Professional Made Easy

HTML Professional Programming Made Easy

CSS Programming Professional Made Easy

Windows 8 Tips for Beginners

**Programming Box Set #79: Android Programming in a Day &
JavaScript Professional Made Easy**

If the links do not work, for whatever reason, you can simply search for these titles on the Amazon website to find them.